BIG-TIME RECORDS

BIG-TIME
FOOTBALL RECORDS

BY THOM STORDEN

CAPSTONE PRESS
a capstone imprint

Published by Capstone Press, an imprint of Capstone.
1710 Roe Crest Drive
North Mankato, Minnesota 56003
capstonepub.com

Copyright © 2022 by Capstone. All rights reserved. No part of this publication may be reproduced in whole or in part, or stored in a retrieval system, or transmitted in any form or by any means, electronic, mechanical, photocopying, recording, or otherwise, without written permission of the publisher.

SPORTS ILLUSTRATED KIDS is a trademark of ABG-SI LLC. Used with permission.

Library of Congress Cataloging-in-Publication Data
Names: Storden, Thom, author.
Title: Big-time football records / by Thom Storden.
Description: North Mankato, Minnesota : Capstone Press, 2022. | Series: Sports illustrated kids big-time records | Includes bibliographical references and index. | Audience: Ages 8–11 | Audience: Grades 4–6
Identifiers: LCCN 2021004300 (print) | LCCN 2021004301 (ebook) | ISBN 9781496695444 (hardcover) | ISBN 9781977159311 (paperback) | ISBN 9781977159007 (ebook PDF)
Subjects: LCSH: Football—Records—Juvenile literature.
Classification: LCC GV950.7 .S76 2022 (print) | LCC GV950.7 (ebook) | DDC 796.33—dc23
LC record available at https://lccn.loc.gov/2021004300
LC ebook record available at https://lccn.loc.gov/2021004301

Summary: Nothing beats the excitement of a player making a fingertip grab to get a game-winning score—except when that big catch sets a new record! Behind every big-time football record is a dramatic story of how a player or team achieved greatness on the gridiron. Strap on your cleats and read all about football's legendary players and teams and their historic record-setting moments.

Editorial Credits
Editor, Aaron Sautter; Designer, Bobbie Nuytten; Media Researcher, Morgan Walters; Production Specialist, Laura Manthe

Image Credits
Associated Press: Associated Press, 43, Harold P. Matosian, 44; Getty Images: Bettmann, 45, Frederick Breedon, 37, Michael Yada, 33, TIMOTHY A. CLARY, 53; Newscom: Daniel Gluskoter/Cal Sport Media, 13, Danielle Beckman, 41, Gary Hershorn, 31, Hahn Lionel/ZUMA Press, 17, Joe Giza/REUTERS, 47, Ray Stubblebine, 42, Stephen Lew/Icon Sportswire, 21; Sports Illustrated: Al Tielemans, 11, 15, 29, 49, top right 51, Bob Rosato, 27, 57, Erick W. Rasco, Cover, 5, 6, 8, 39, Heinz Kluetmeier, 19, John Biever, 25, top left 51, John D. Hanlon, top left 35, John Iacono, 59, Neil Leifer, top right 35, 50, Robert Beck, 23, Walter Iooss Jr., 55

All records and statistics in this book are current through the 2020 season.

TABLE OF CONTENTS

WORDS IN **BOLD** APPEAR IN THE GLOSSARY.

RECORDS ARE MADE TO BE BROKEN

Football is a marvelous game. Football players have amazing speed and power. The passing, receiving, rushing, and tackling thrill huge crowds. Stadiums echo with the cheers of roaring fans. Even the ball is **unique**. No other sport is quite like football.

One of the best things about the game is watching the breathtaking athletes and their performances on the field. And just when you think you've seen it all—another star tops it. That must be why the old saying, "Records are made to be broken," rings true.

But for a few moments, before they're broken again, we can enjoy the record-setting accomplishments in the sport. From the greatest Hail Mary touchdowns and fourth quarter comebacks to bone-crushing **sacks** and Super Bowl rings—the best of the best is right here at your fingertips. Get ready to be thrilled and amazed by football's biggest record-setting plays and playmakers.

Baltimore Ravens wide receiver Miles Boykin attempts to catch a touchdown pass against the Tennessee Titans.

Chapter One

BIG-TIME PASSERS

When the center snaps the ball, 22 players on the field burst into action. But who holds the ball in those first moments after it's snapped? Who hands it off or throws it? Who sneaks the ball through the line to get that final yard? That's right—the quarterback. Many of football's most amazing moments have featured the greatest signal callers in the biz.

On February 7, 2021, Tom Brady led the Tampa Bay Buccaneers to win his seventh career Super Bowl championship.

Brees or Brady?

Brees or Brady? Brady or Brees? You really can't go wrong either way. Having played nearly identical years as pros, Drew Brees and Tom Brady have a lot in common. Brady came into the National Football League (NFL) in 2000. Brees arrived in 2001. Both have had incredibly successful careers.

Football is a very physical sport. It wears down the body of every player. Quarterbacks often take some of the most violent hits. So for Brady and Brees to continue playing as elite quarterbacks into their 40s is an amazing achievement. Both QBs are big-time winners.

Career Touchdown Passes

RANK	PLAYER	TD PASSES	YEARS ACTIVE	TEAMS
1	Tom Brady	581*	2000–present	Patriots, Buccaneers
2	Drew Brees	571	2001–2020	Chargers, Saints
3	Peyton Manning	539	1998–2015	Colts, Broncos
4	Brett Favre	508	1991–2010	Falcons, Packers, Jets, Vikings
5	Philip Rivers	421	2004–2020	Chargers, Colts

*Stats listed are through the 2020 season.

Drew Brees was born and raised in Texas. He played college ball at Purdue University in Indiana. The star passer played his first five NFL seasons for the San Diego Chargers. In 2006 he was acquired by the New Orleans Saints. At exactly 6 feet (183 centimeters) tall, Brees wasn't a huge player. He wasn't much of a runner either. But Brees had a golden arm and excellent vision. His understanding of the game was genius. He was a clutch player when the game was on the line.

After 20 years in the NFL, Drew Brees retired as one of the greatest QBs of all time after the 2020 season.

Injured Stars

Tom Brady and Drew Brees both enjoyed long and mostly healthy careers. But like many players, they had their share of injuries. Brady suffered a bad knee injury in the first game of the 2008 season. It caused him to miss the rest of that season. He has also had several shoulder, ankle, foot, and hand injuries. Brees' most serious injury was in 2019. He missed five games due to a torn thumb **ligament** in his throwing hand. Both quarterbacks have also endured **concussions**.

Tom Brady was born and raised in California. He played college ball at the University of Michigan. He was chosen in the sixth round of the 2000 NFL Draft by the New England Patriots. Brady played in only one game as a **rookie**. But the next year he led the Pats to win the Super Bowl. He led his team to five more Super Bowl titles during his time in New England. In 2020 Brady started a new chapter in his career when he signed with the Tampa Bay Buccaneers. He added to his legendary status by leading the Bucs to a Super Bowl title that year.

Brees vs. Brady

	TOM BRADY*	DREW BREES
Seasons	2000-present	2001-2020
Teams	Patriots, Buccaneers	Chargers, Saints
Completions/ Attempts Percentage	64.0%	67.7%
Yards Passing	79,204	80,358
Touchdowns/ Interceptions	581/191	571/243
Rushing Touchdowns	25	25
Fumbles	126	112
Times Sacked	521	420
Longest TD Pass	99 yards	98 yards
Regular Season Wins–Losses	230–69	172–114
Fourth Quarter Comebacks	39	36
Playoff Record	34–11	9–9
Super Bowl Titles	7	1
Super Bowl MVPs	5	1

*Stats listed are through the 2020 season.

Manning of the Hour

When Peyton Manning retired after the 2015 season, he went out on top. He had recently led the Denver Broncos to a Super Bowl victory. And in doing so, he became the first quarterback to win championships with two different teams. When Manning hung up his cleats, he held most of the NFL's big-time passing records. Most completions, most yards, most touchdown passes—he owned them all.

Manning had previously played 13 successful seasons with the Indianapolis Colts. But in 2011, he sat out the entire season with a serious neck injury. Many fans thought he might never play again. But Manning wasn't ready to hang up his cleats yet.

Touchdown Passes, Single Season

RANK	PLAYER	TEAM	SEASON	TOUCHDOWN PASSES
1	Peyton Manning	Broncos	2013	55
2	Patrick Mahomes	Chiefs	2018	50
3	Tom Brady	Patriots	2007	50
4	Peyton Manning	Colts	2004	49
5	Dan Marino	Dolphins	1984	48

Peyton Manning won the NFL Most Valuable Player (MVP) award five times. No other player has won it more than three times.

Peyton Manning led the Indianapolis Colts to defeat the Chicago Bears and win the championship title in Super Bowl XLI on February 4, 2007.

After a successful surgery and months of **therapy**, Manning began his second act with Denver in 2012. He quickly showed that he was still one of the best QBs in the league. That first year he threw for more than 4,600 yards and tossed 37 TDs for the Broncos. Then came his magical 2013 season. Just two years after his injury, Manning set a record with an amazing 55 touchdown passes for the Broncos. Four Broncos receivers each caught at least 10 TDs, including Demaryius Thomas (14), Julius Thomas (12), Eric Decker (11), and Wes Welker (10).

But Manning did much more than throw a lot of TDs. He was also the captain of the comeback. Brees and Brady have both played longer than Manning did. But they still trail him when it comes to clutch wins. A master of the last minute, Manning led his teams to 43 fourth quarter come-from-behind wins. It didn't matter if it was with the Indianapolis Colts or the Denver Broncos. Manning was determined to pull it out for the win.

4th Quarter QB Comebacks

RANK	PLAYER	4TH QUARTER COMEBACKS	YEARS ACTIVE	TEAMS
1	Peyton Manning	43	1998–2015	Colts, Broncos
2	Tom Brady	39*	2000–present	Patriots, Buccaneers
3	Drew Brees	36	2001–2020	Chargers, Saints
4	Ben Roethlisberger	35*	2004–present	Steelers
5	Johnny Unitas	34	1956–1973	Colts, Chargers

*Stats listed are through the 2020 season.

Peyton Manning had seven fourth quarter comeback wins in 2009. The record for most fourth quarter comebacks in a season is eight. Detroit Lions QB Matthew Stafford set the record in 2016.

Peyton Manning's record 55th touchdown pass came against the Oakland Raiders on December 29, 2013. He also set the season record for most passing yards (5,477) on the same play.

Gridiron Man

Brett Favre was a gambler. He took plenty of chances. He forced passes into tight spaces and ran when it wasn't safe. He rarely took the easy way out. Starting 321 **consecutive** games at quarterback was definitely not easy. In fact, no one has even come close to matching that number in pro football.

The "Iron Man" of pro baseball was Cal Ripken, Jr. He played 2,632 straight games. A.C. Green played 1,192 games in a row for the pro basketball record. Doug Jarvis played 964 straight pro hockey games. Jeff Gordon started 797 auto races. These are all impressive marks. But none of these people faced 300+ pound (136+ kilogram) linemen ready to pound them to the ground the way Favre did. Football is a crushing game. Brett Favre was a survivor.

Most Consecutive Starts at Quarterback
(Regular Season and Playoffs Combined)

RANK	PLAYER	GAMES	DATES	TEAMS
1	Brett Favre	321	9/27/1992–12/5/2010	Packers, Jets, Vikings
2	Philip Rivers	252	9/11/2006–1/3/2021	Chargers, Colts
3	Peyton Manning	227	9/6/1998–1/2/2011	Colts
4	Eli Manning	222	11/21/2004–11/23/2017	Giants
5	Matt Ryan	163	12/20/2009–10/20/2019	Falcons

Brett Favre (#4) was one of the toughest quarterbacks to ever play in the NFL.

Brett Favre holds the NFL record for **interceptions** with 336. No other QB has reached 300. The next closest is George Blanda, who played from 1949 to 1975 and threw 277 interceptions.

Young and Famous

Good quarterbacks have great arms. They can make pinpoint passes to receivers who make toe-tapping catches on the sidelines. They can zing bullets over the middle. And they can loft soft fade routes into the corner of the end zone.

But the best quarterbacks have more than arm skill. They're great leaders too. The best of the best learn to lead even at a young age. In 2020 Patrick Mahomes became the second-youngest quarterback to win the Super Bowl. Mahomes was also named the Super Bowl MVP after leading the Kansas City Chiefs to a come-from-behind win over the San Francisco 49ers.

But Mahomes wasn't the first young QB to lead his team to a championship. Ben Roethlisberger first suited up for the Pittsburgh Steelers in 2004. In his second season, he helped his team win Super Bowl XL. He was the youngest QB ever to win it all.

Youngest Quarterbacks to Win the Super Bowl

RANK	PLAYER	AGE	SUPER BOWL RESULT	YEAR
1	Ben Roethlisberger	23 years and 11 months	Steelers over Seahawks, 21–10	2006
2	Patrick Mahomes	24 years and 4 months	Chiefs over 49ers, 31–20	2020
3	Tom Brady	24 years and 6 months	Patriots over Rams, 20–17	2002
4	Russell Wilson	25 years and 2 months	Seahawks over Broncos, 43–8	2014
5	Joe Namath	25 years and 7 months	Jets over Colts, 16–7	1969

Patrick Mahomes (right) became the youngest player ever to win both a Super Bowl and an NFL MVP award.

Chapter Two

BIG-TIME RECEIVERS

Fast and Fruitful

Jerry Rice was a flash of lightning on the field. The slim, speedy receiver spent most of his glory-filled career with the San Francisco 49ers. In 16 seasons with the red and gold, Rice teamed up with two different Hall of Fame QBs in Joe Montana and Steve Young. He helped the Niners win three Super Bowls, and he set numerous records. His numbers kept going up during the last four years of his career with the Oakland Raiders and Seattle Seahawks.

Most Career Receptions

RANK	PLAYER	RECEPTIONS	YEARS ACTIVE	TEAM
1	Jerry Rice	1,549	1985–2004	49ers, Raiders, Seahawks
2	Larry Fitzgerald	1,432*	2004–present	Cardinals
3	Tony Gonzalez	1,325	1997–2013	Chiefs, Chargers
4	Jason Witten	1,228	2003–2020	Cowboys, Raiders
5	Marvin Harrison	1,102	1996–2008	Colts

*Stats listed are through the 2020 season.

San Francisco 49ers legend Jerry Rice celebrated after scoring a touchdown against the Denver Broncos in Super Bowl XXIV in 1990.

For years, Rice's astonishing 1,549 career receptions seemed like an untouchable record. But Larry Fitzgerald of the Arizona Cardinals racked up season after season of greatness. Fitzgerald has never won a Super Bowl. The Cardinals weren't as consistent as the 49ers were during Rice's time. But Fitz endures. After 1,432 catches in 16 seasons, he may still have a chance to top the great Rice.

Catch Master

In 2018 Michael Thomas of the New Orleans Saints led the NFL with 125 catches. The wide receiver was rewarded during the offseason. He was given the richest contract in pro football history for a non-quarterback (5 years, $100 million).

Thomas wasn't about to get lazy after his big payday. Instead he went back to work more determined than ever. In 2019 Thomas and his quarterbacks, Drew Brees and Teddy Bridgewater, put on a show. The Saints threw the ball all over the field, and they threw to Thomas often. By the end of the regular season, Thomas had caught an astounding 149 passes and set a new NFL record.

Most Receptions in a Season

RANK	PLAYER	RECEPTIONS	SEASON	TEAM
1	Michael Thomas	149	2019	Saints
2	Marvin Harrison	143	2002	Colts
3	Antonio Brown	136	2015	Steelers
3	Julio Jones	136	2015	Falcons
5	Antonio Brown	129	2014	Steelers

Michael Thomas's uncle is Keyshawn Johnson, an 11-year NFL veteran and three-time Pro Bowl receiver.

Michael Thomas (#13) finished the 2019 season with an NFL record-smashing 149 catches.

Mr. Consistency

Julio Jones's birth name is Quintorris Lopez Jones. Although he wears a number (#11) usually used by a quarterback, he's one of the NFL's most talented receivers. On one play, Jones can show the grace of a ballet dancer, toeing the sideline while hauling in a fingertip catch. On the next play, he'll steamroll a defensive back like a runaway monster truck. He'll often juke defenders and blow past safeties to get open downfield.

But what makes Julio Jones truly unique is his ability to play great football game in and game out. His stats reflect that. Since being drafted out of the University of Alabama in 2011 by the Atlanta Falcons, Jones has come to play. As a rookie, he caught 8 touchdowns and showed great promise. Since then, Jones has made the Pro Bowl almost every season he's played. He's also become the all-time leader in yards per game, with a 95.5 mark.

Most Receiving Yards Per Game

RANK	PLAYER	YARDS PER GAME	YEARS ACTIVE	TEAMS
1	Julio Jones	95.5*	2011–present	Falcons
2	Calvin Johnson	86.1	2007–2015	Lions
3	Michael Thomas	85.0*	2016–present	Saints
4	Antonio Brown	84.5*	2010–present	Steelers, Patriots, Buccaneers
5	Odell Beckham Jr.	83.3*	2014–present	Giants, Browns

*Stats listed are through the 2020 season.

Julio Jones made an acrobatic catch against the New England Patriots in Super Bowl LI in 2017.

In 2019 Julio Jones passed Roddy White to become the Falcons' all-time leading receiver. The two are the only receivers in Falcons history to go over 10,000 yards total.

Rookie Sensation

Randy Moss had athletic skills rarely seen on the field. Because of his seemingly mutant abilities, he was given the nickname "The Freak." Defensive backs didn't have much of a chance against him one on one. He was tall, nimble, insanely fast, and had superhero-like jumping ability. Growing up in his home state of West Virginia, Moss was even better known as a high-flying and rim-rocking basketball player. In 1995 he was named West Virginia's Mr. Basketball, an honor given to the top high school player in the state.

Moss received plenty of college basketball scholarship offers. But he decided to focus on football. Gridiron fans were happy he did. Just three years after graduating high school, Moss was a rookie star with the Minnesota Vikings. During his first season in 1998, he caught a rookie record of 17 touchdowns while helping the Vikings finish with the best record in the league. He also finished as a first team All-Pro. Moss's first pro season would lay the blueprint for a Hall of Fame career.

As a member of the Patriots, Randy Moss caught four touchdowns on November 18, 2007, against the Buffalo Bills. It was the most he caught in a pro game. As a college player at Marshall University, Moss once caught five touchdowns in a game against Ball State.

Randy Moss's record 17 touchdown catches helped the 1998 Minnesota Vikings become one of the highest scoring teams in history.

Perhaps Moss's finest season came in 2007 while playing for the New England Patriots. With legendary QB Tom Brady slinging passes, Moss caught an NFL single season record of 23 touchdowns. Unbelievably, the Pats were **upset** 17–14 by the New York Giants in Super Bowl XLII—the only loss of their season. But for Moss, it was a season for the ages.

Most TD Receptions, Single Season

RANK	PLAYER	TOUCHDOWNS	YEAR	TEAM
1	Randy Moss	23	2007	Patriots
2	Jerry Rice	22	1987	49ers
3	Davante Adams	18	2020	Packers
3	Mark Clayton	18	1984	Dolphins
3	Sterling Sharpe	18	1994	Packers

Most TD Receptions, Single Game

RANK	PLAYER	TEAM VS. OPPONENT	DATE	TDs
1	Jerry Rice	49ers vs. Falcons	October 14, 1990	5
1	Kellen Winslow Sr.	Chargers vs. Raiders	November 22, 1981	5
1	Bob Shaw	Cardinals vs. Colts	October 2, 1950	5
38 players tied with 4 TD receptions in a single game				

With his record 23 touchdown grabs, Randy Moss helped lead the New England Patriots to an incredible 16–0 regular season record in 2007.

Randy Moss's son, Thaddeus, was a tight end for the Louisiana State University (LSU) Tigers. On January 13, 2020, LSU beat Clemson 42–25 in the national championship game. It was the perfect way to cap off an undefeated season. In that game, Thaddeus Moss caught two touchdowns.

Chapter Three

BIG-TIME RUSHERS

Relentless Rushing

Think about what it takes to gain just a single yard in an NFL game. Muscular and vicious defenders are waiting to make a tackle. To move the ball forward, it takes speed. It takes power. It takes vision. It takes toughness. And it definitely takes fearlessness.

Emmitt Smith had all of those qualities. The longtime NFL running back played his best seasons in the 1990s for the Dallas Cowboys. After a fantastic college career with the University of Florida, Smith was drafted by the Cowboys in 1990. In his rookie season, Smith rushed for 937 yards and 11 touchdowns. It was a good start, but Smith was just warming up.

Most Rushing Yards, Single Game

RANK	PLAYER	TEAM VS. OPPONENT	DATE	RUSHING YARDS
1	Adrian Peterson	Vikings vs. Chargers	Nov. 4, 2007	296
2	Jamal Lewis	Ravens vs. Browns	Sept. 14, 2003	295
3	Jerome Harrison	Browns vs. Chiefs	Dec. 20, 2009	286
4	Corey Dillon	Bengals vs. Broncos	Oct. 22, 2000	278
5	Walter Payton	Bears vs. Vikings	Nov. 20, 1977	275

Emmitt Smith was a fearless running back for the Dallas Cowboys from 1990 to 2002.

Starting in 1991, Smith broke the 1,000-yard barrier each season for the next 11 years. He was a workhorse running back, but he wasn't flashy. He gained yards by rushing into the teeth of defenses over and over. And he kept at it until defensive players made mistakes or wore down.

The Cowboys had a talented offense. Along with Smith the team also featured star quarterback Troy Aikman and receiver Michael Irvin. The Cowboys' offensive line was also huge and powerful and deserves a lot of credit for opening holes for Smith to run through.

But that didn't take away from Smith's talent. He was a good blocker for Aikman and was also a fine receiver out of the backfield. He tallied more than 500 receptions and gained more than 3,000 receiving yards during his career. With Smith leading the way, the Cowboys captured three Super Bowl titles in the 1990s.

Smith closed out his career playing two years for the Arizona Cardinals. By the end of his 15-season career, he had rushed for 18,355 yards. It was enough to replace Chicago Bears great Walter Payton at the top spot of the all-time rushing list.

Most Rushing Yards, Career

RANK	PLAYER	RUSHING YARDS	YEARS	TEAMS
1	Emmitt Smith	18,355	1990–2004	Cowboys, Cardinals
2	Walter Payton	16,726	1975–1987	Bears
3	Frank Gore	16,000*	2005–present	49ers, Colts, Dolphins, Bills, Jets
4	Barry Sanders	15,269	1989–1998	Lions
5	Adrian Peterson	14,820*	2007–present	Vikings, Saints, Cardinals, Washington, Lions

*Stats listed are through the 2020 season.

Emmitt Smith and receiver Michael Irvin celebrated after winning Super Bowl XXVII in 1993.

Adrian Peterson was born in Palestine, Texas, in 1985. His favorite team and player were the Cowboys and Emmitt Smith.

Elite Rushers Only

A long-standing mark of excellence in the NFL has been the number 1,000. If a player breaks the 1,000-yard barrier in a single season, he's said to have had a very good year. If a running back plays in all 16 regular season games, he would have to average 62.5 yards per game to hit 1,000 yards. But these players face a lot of obstacles that stand in their way, including stingy defenses, bad weather, and injuries. Getting to 1,000 yards isn't easy.

When a player rushes for 2,000 yards in a season, it's considered an epic achievement. It's so rare that only eight running backs in the history of pro football have accomplished it.

The all-time single-season rushing leader is Eric Dickerson. In 1984 he ran for 2,105 yards for the Los Angeles Rams. Dickerson had an upright running style built on speed. At 6 feet, 3 inches (191 centimeters) he was taller than a typical running back. But with his long legs he had a gliding stride that covered distance quickly.

Single Season "2,000 Yard Club"

RANK	PLAYER	YARDS	YEAR	TEAM
1	Eric Dickerson	2,105	1984	Rams
2	Adrian Peterson	2,097	2012	Vikings
3	Jamal Lewis	2,066	2003	Ravens
4	Barry Sanders	2,053	1997	Lions
5	Derrick Henry	2,027	2020	Titans
6	Terrell Davis	2,008	1998	Broncos
7	Chris Johnson	2,006	2009	Titans
8	O.J. Simpson	2,003	1973	Bills

Eric Dickerson broke O.J. Simpson's single-season rushing record against the Houston Oilers on December 9, 1984.

O.J. Simpson was the first person to break the 2,000-yard barrier in 1973. His effort was especially impressive since at that time the NFL only played 14 regular season games. Simpson also played for the Buffalo Bills. Their home games in Buffalo, New York, were often played in cold weather on a slippery field.

Most running backs also strive to win the league's rushing title each season. One of pro football's earliest rushing heroes was Jim Brown. Playing for the Cleveland Browns from 1957–1965, Brown led the league in rushing yardage in eight of his nine seasons. No other rusher has led the league more than four times—half as often as Brown.

Most Rushing Titles

RANK	PLAYER	RUSHING TITLES	TEAM/YEARS
1	Jim Brown	8	Browns, 1957–1961, 1963–1965
2	Steve Van Buren	4	Eagles, 1945, 1947–1949
2	O.J. Simpson	4	Bills, 1972, 1973, 1975, 1976
2	Eric Dickerson	4	Rams, 1983, 1984, 1986; Colts, 1988
2	Emmitt Smith	4	Cowboys, 1991–1993, 1995
2	Barry Sanders	4	Lions, 1990, 1994, 1996, 1997

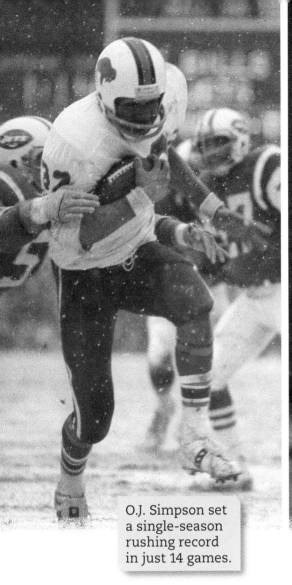

O.J. Simpson set a single-season rushing record in just 14 games.

Jim Brown won the league season rushing title a record eight times.

In Eric Dickerson's record-breaking, 2,105-yard season in 1984, he averaged 131.6 yards rushing per game. Jim Brown's best yards-per-game average was 133.1 in 1963. In O.J. Simpson's 2,000-yard season of 1973, he averaged a whopping 143.1 yards per game.

The Long Run

During a game in 2018, Tennessee Titans running back Derrick Henry made one of the most amazing runs in NFL history. The Titans led the Jacksonville Jaguars 7–2 in the second quarter. Henry's team had the ball, but its back was against its own goal line. The ball sat on the 1-yard line. It was first and ten.

Quarterback Marcus Mariota called out the signals. Lined up seven yards deep in the end zone, Henry popped up and took the handoff from Mariota following the snap. There was a pileup of players at the goal line, but Henry scooted through the line off a block from the left tackle.

In a flash, Henry saw some daylight. At the 20-yard line, he stiff-armed Jaguars cornerback A.J. Bouye. Then he picked up steam. At midfield, the Jags' Leon Jacobs tried to tackle Henry but was also stiff-armed. The crowd began to roar.

Longest Rush from Scrimmage

RANK	PLAYER	TEAM	SEASON	YARDS
1	Derrick Henry	Titans	2018	99
1	Tony Dorsett	Cowboys	1982	99
3	Ahman Green	Packers	2003	98
4	Lamar Miller	Texans	2018	97
4	Lamar Miller	Dolphins	2014	97
4	Bob Gage	Steelers	1949	97
4	Andy Uram	Packers	1939	97

Derrick Henry's epic 99-yard run in 2018 tied Tony Dorsett's record run made in 1982.

Henry passed the Jags' 30-yard line, and then the 25. At the 20-yard line, Jags linebacker Myles Jack had a chance to bring Henry down. Henry stuck out his hand one more time, knocking Jack aside with another epic stiff-arm. Arriving in the end zone, Henry's teammates mobbed him in celebration. Henry had run for a 99-yard touchdown. He'd just tied the record for longest run in league history.

Tony Dorsett of the Dallas Cowboys was the first and only running back to run for a 99-yard touchdown before Derrick Henry. Dorsett made his run in a Cowboys' loss to the Minnesota Vikings in the final game of the 1982 regular season.

Action Jackson

When quarterback Lamar Jackson broke into the NFL in 2018 with the Baltimore Ravens, he reminded many fans of someone else. That player was Michael Vick, who had officially retired only the year before. Vick was arguably the best rushing quarterback that the NFL had ever seen.

In 2001, Vick was drafted by the Atlanta Falcons. His scrambling style of play left fans breathless. In 2006 he became the first pro QB to break the 1,000-yard mark in a single season, rushing for 1,039 yards.

Fast-forward to 2019. Lamar Jackson had just come off a successful rookie season in Baltimore. His second season, though, would be one for the record books. Jackson proved to be nearly unstoppable, leading the Ravens to a league-best 14–2 record. He threw a league-leading 36 touchdowns (and only six interceptions). But Jackson was even more impressive with his running. He rushed for 1,206 yards on the season, besting Vick's mark for quarterbacks. For his efforts Jackson was named the 2019 NFL MVP. He kept up his amazing performance the next year with 1,005 rushing yards in 2020.

Single Season Rushing Yards, Quarterback

RANK	PLAYER	TEAM	YEAR	YARDS RUSHING
1	Lamar Jackson	Ravens	2019	1,206
2	Michael Vick	Falcons	2006	1,039
3	Lamar Jackson	Ravens	2020	1,005
4	Bobby Douglass	Bears	1972	968
5	Randall Cunningham	Eagles	1990	942

Lamar Jackson set the NFL on fire in 2019 with his quarterback rushing record of 1,206 yards.

Chapter Four

BIG-TIME DEFENDERS

Sack Masters

One of the most exciting defensive plays in football is the quarterback sack. The sack has a lot to offer: the clash of the offensive and defensive lines, the thrill of a chase, the power of a majestic tackle. It takes more than muscle to bring down a QB. It takes cunning, speed, and **anticipation**.

Career Sacks

RANK	PLAYER	SACKS	YEARS	TEAMS
1	Bruce Smith	200.0	1985–2003	Bills, Washington
2	Reggie White	198.0	1985–2000	Eagles, Packers, Panthers
3	Kevin Green	160.0	1985–1999	Rams, Steelers, Panthers, 49ers
4	Julius Peppers	159.5	2002–2018	Panthers, Bears, Packers
5	Chris Doleman	150.5	1985–1999	Vikings, Falcons, 49ers

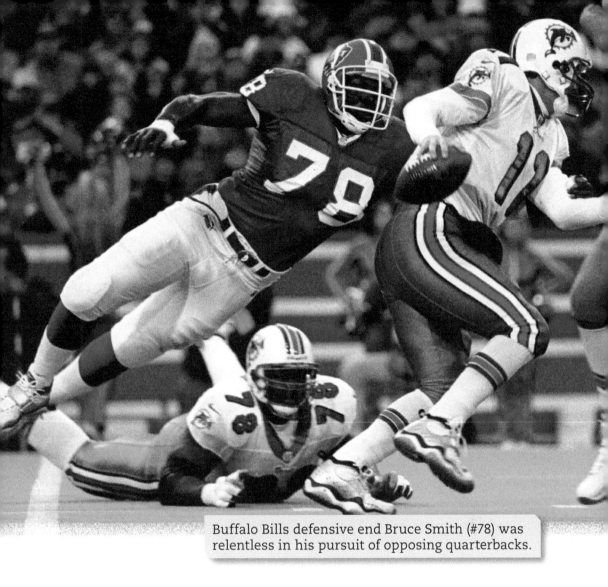

Buffalo Bills defensive end Bruce Smith (#78) was relentless in his pursuit of opposing quarterbacks.

The NFL began officially recording sacks in 1982. By chance, the top three sack masters on the career sacks list began playing in 1985. Bruce Smith, Reggie White, and Kevin Greene were all talented defensive linemen who had long careers with multiple teams.

Michael Strahan played his whole career with the New York Giants. He was a defensive end in the classic mold of big, powerful, and quick sack masters. In the final game of the 2001 season, Strahan sat at 21.5 sacks. In the final minutes of the game, he sped by the offensive line to sack QB Brett Favre. The move set the record for most sacks in a season with 22.5.

Single Season Sacks

RANK	PLAYER	TEAM	YEAR	SACKS
1	Michael Strahan	Giants	2001	22.5
2	Jared Allen	Vikings	2011	22.0
2	Mark Gastineau	Jets	1984	22.0
2	Justin Houston	Chiefs	2014	22.0
5	Chris Doleman	Vikings	1989	21.0
5	Reggie White	Eagles	1987	21.0

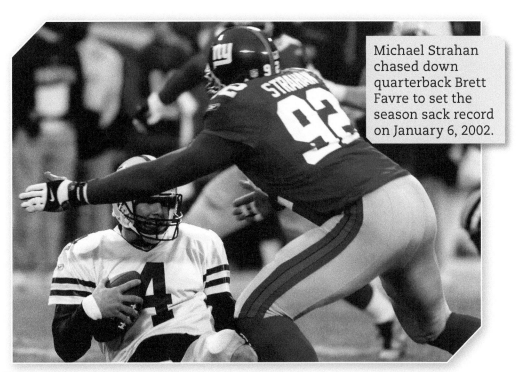

Michael Strahan chased down quarterback Brett Favre to set the season sack record on January 6, 2002.

Derrick Thomas was a dominant linebacker for the Kansas City Chiefs in the 1990s. During a game in 1990, he put on an amazing defensive performance. Thomas racked up an incredible seven sacks of Seattle Seahawks QB Dave Krieg. But in spite of Thomas's efforts, the Seahawks pulled off a 17–16 win on a late Krieg TD pass.

Single Game Sacks

RANK	PLAYER	TEAM VS. OPPONENT	DATE	SACKS
1	Derrick Thomas	Chiefs vs. Seahawks	11-11-1990	7
2	Adrian Clayborn	Falcons vs. Cowboys	11-12-2017	6
2	Derrick Thomas	Chiefs vs. Raiders	9-6-1998	6
2	Osi Umenyiora	Giants vs. Eagles	9-30-2007	6
2	Fred Dean	49ers vs. Saints	11-13-1983	6

Derrick Thomas terrorized opposing quarterbacks for 11 NFL seasons.

Ball Hawks

The defense's main job is to get the ball back for their own team. How do defenders get it back? They can stop an opposing offense on downs, cause and recover a fumble, or intercept a pass. Good defensive backs or safeties are just as skilled at catching passes as talented receivers.

Dick "Night Train" Lane set the mark for most interceptions in a season way back in 1952 with 14. Amazingly, Lane pulled off the feat during his rookie season with the Los Angeles Rams. Night Train was inducted into the Hall of Fame in 1974.

Dick "Night Train" Lane intercepted a pass against the Green Bay Packers on December 7, 1952.

Single Season Interceptions

RANK	PLAYER	INTERCEPTIONS	YEAR	TEAM
1	Dick Lane	14	1952	Rams
2	Lester Hayes	13	1980	Raiders
2	Dan Sandifer	13	1948	Washington
2	Spec Sanders	13	1950	Yanks
5	9 players tied with 12 interceptions			

Paul Krause (#22) intercepted a pass against the Dallas Cowboys on October 20, 1968.

One of the greatest defensive pass catchers ever seen in the pros was Paul Krause. Krause was a constant threat to opposing quarterbacks. He picked off 81 passes in his 16 seasons in the NFL. Krause also appeared in four Super Bowls with the Minnesota Vikings, notching three interceptions in the playoffs.

The best interceptors can also take it the other way and score for their own team. An interception returned for a touchdown, known as a "**pick six**," was the specialty of Rod Woodson. The fierce safety played 10 seasons with the Pittsburgh Steelers before joining the Baltimore Ravens toward the end of his career. Woodson and linebacker Ray Lewis led the Ravens to win Super Bowl XXXV in 2001. Many fans consider that Ravens team to be the best defensive unit in NFL history. For his career, Woodson had an impressive 12 pick six interception returns.

Career Interceptions (INTs)

RANK	PLAYER	INTs	YEARS	TEAMS
1	Paul Krause	81	1964–1979	Washington, Vikings
2	Emlen Tunnell	79	1948–1961	Giants, Packers
3	Rod Woodson	71	1987–2003	Steelers, 49ers, Ravens, Raiders
4	Dick Lane	68	1952–1965	Rams, Cardinals, Lions
5	Ken Riley	65	1969–1983	Bengals
5	Charles Woodson	65	1998–2015	Raiders, Packers

Career Interceptions (INTs) Returned for Touchdown

RANK	PLAYER	INTs	YEARS	TEAMS
1	Rod Woodson	12	1987–2003	Steelers, 49ers, Ravens, Raiders
2	Charles Woodson	11	1998–2015	Raiders, Packers
2	Darren Sharper	11	1997–2010	Packers, Vikings, Saints
4	Aqib Talib	10	2008–2019	Buccaneers, Patriots, Broncos, Rams
5	3 players tied with 9			

Rod Woodson waved to fans after scoring a pick six touchdown against the Tennessee Titans in 1999.

Chapter Five

BIG-TIME SPECIAL TEAMS PLAYERS

Just for Kicks

The kickoff is one of the most routine plays in football. Its main function is to get a game started with one team kicking the ball to the other. But kickoffs can sometimes lead to the most thrilling plays in the game. Some of the longest-scoring plays come from kicks that are returned for touchdowns.

Josh Cribbs was an extraordinary kick returner for the Cleveland Browns. During his first five seasons, from 2005–2009, he returned at least one kick for a touchdown each season. The highlight of Cribbs's career came in 2009, when he returned three kickoffs for TDs.

Career Kick Returns for Touchdowns

RANK	PLAYER	TDs	YEARS	TEAMS
1	Josh Cribbs	8	2005–2014	Browns, Jets, Colts
1	Leon Washington	8	2006–2014	Jets, Seahawks, Patriots, Titans
1	Cordarrelle Patterson	8*	2013–present	Vikings, Raiders, Patriots, Bears

*Stats listed are through the 2020 season.

Leon Washington joins Cribbs atop the leaderboard with eight career kick returns for touchdowns. Washington returned three kicks for TDs for the New York Jets in 2007. In 2010 Washington did the same thing for the Seattle Seahawks.

There would be no kickoffs without the kickers. There would also be no field goals or extra points. Adam Vinatieri is considered to be the gold standard when it comes to kickers. With 599 completed field goals, he's had more success than any other kicker. Vinatieri has also helped kick his teams to four Super Bowl titles, including two game-winning kicks in Super Bowls XXXVI and XXXVIII.

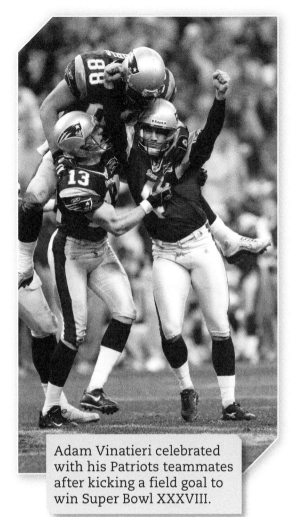

Adam Vinatieri celebrated with his Patriots teammates after kicking a field goal to win Super Bowl XXXVIII.

Field Goals Made

RANK	PLAYER	FG	YEARS	TEAMS
1	Adam Vinatieri	599	1996–2019	Patriots, Colts
2	Morten Andersen	565	1982–2007	Saints, Falcons, Giants, Chiefs, Vikings
3	Gary Anderson	538	1982–2004	Steelers, Eagles, 49ers, Vikings, Titans
4	Jason Hanson	495	1992–2012	Lions
5	John Carney	478	1988–2010	Buccaneers, Rams, Chargers, Saints, Jaguars, Chiefs, Giants

Many Happy Returns

Devin Hester was an electric punt returner. He was fast as the wind and could change directions like a salmon mid-stream. Hester was a fan-favorite during his 11-year career, mostly with the Chicago Bears. With 14 punt returns for touchdowns to his name, Hester is far and away the punt return king.

Punters don't always get a lot of credit in the NFL. But booting the ball consistently is a big factor in winning the war of field position. No one has boomed more punts in the NFL than Jeff Feagles. He spent most of his career on the East Coast, playing for the New York Giants, Philadelphia Eagles, and New England Patriots. He also played for the Seattle Seahawks and Arizona Cardinals in his 22-season career.

Old Man Blanda

George Blanda holds the record for most seasons in the NFL with 26. Blanda played for four different teams and was multitalented, playing as a kicker, punter, and quarterback.

Career Punt Returns for Touchdowns

RANK	PLAYER	TDs	YEARS	TEAMS
1	Devin Hester	14	2006–2016	Bears, Falcons, Ravens, Seahawks
2	Eric Metcalf	10	1989–2002	Browns, Falcons, Chargers, Cardinals, Panthers, Washington, Packers
3	Brian Mitchell	9	1990–2003	Washington, Eagles, Giants
4	Jack Christiansen	8	1951–1958	Lions
4	Desmond Howard	8	1992–2002	Washington, Jaguars, Packers, Raiders, Lions
4	Rick Upchurch	8	1975–1983	Broncos

With his slick moves and blinding speed, Devin Hester (#23) often outran his opponents during punt returns.

Jeff Feagles spent 22 years in the NFL punting balls for five different teams.

Career Punts

RANK	PLAYER	PUNTS	YEARS	TEAMS
1	Jeff Feagles	1,713	1988–2009	Patriots, Eagles, Cardinals, Seahawks, Giants
2	Shane Lechler	1,444	2000–2017	Raiders, Texans
3	Sean Landeta	1,401	1985–2005	Giants, Rams, Buccaneers, Packers, Eagles
4	Andy Lee	1,348*	2004–present	49ers, Browns, Panthers, Cardinals
5	Brad Maynard	1,339	1997–2011	Giants, Bears, Browns

*Stats listed are through the 2020 season.

Chapter Six

GREATNESS ON THE GRIDIRON

Good to Be King

Tom Brady and the New England Patriots enjoyed an incredibly successful 20-season run. From 2000–2019, the legendary quarterback led the Pats to success time and time again. In Brady's second year with the team, the Pats upset the heavily favored St. Louis Rams to win Super Bowl XXXVI. Over the years Brady led the Patriots to five more Super Bowl championships.

New England's coach, Bill Belichick, also deserves much of the credit. Belichick built a winner out of the Patriots after the **franchise** struggled for much of its history. Since he took over, the Patriots have consistently been one of the best teams in the NFL. But Belichick struggled during his first coaching gig with the Cleveland Browns. In five seasons with the Browns, Belichick put together just one winning season.

Most Super Bowl Titles

RANK	PLAYER	TITLES
1	Tom Brady	7*
2	Charles Haley	5
3	many players	4

*Stats listed are through the 2020 season.

Together, quarterback Tom Brady (left) and coach Bill Belichick helped the New England Patriots become one of the most successful teams in NFL history.

Winningest Coaches

RANK	COACH	SEASONS	YEARS	WINS	TEAMS
1	Don Shula	33	1963–1995	328	Colts, Dolphins
2	George Halas	40	1920–1967	318	Staleys, Bears
3	Bill Belichick	25	1991–2020	280*	Browns, Patriots
4	Tom Landry	29	1960–1988	250	Cowboys
5	Curly Lambeau	33	1921–1953	226	Packers, Cardinals, Washington

*Stats listed are through the 2020 season.

The Patriots are tied with the Pittsburgh Steelers for all-time leader in Super Bowl victories. Both teams have won six titles. The Steelers had a great **dynasty** during the 1970s. The team won four of their championships with stars like QB Terry Bradshaw, running back Franco Harris, and the "Steel Curtain" defense. Pittsburgh won two more titles with another stingy defense and quarterback Ben Roethlisberger in 2006 and 2009.

Most Super Bowl Titles

RANK

1	**Pittsburgh Steelers** 6 Super Bowl Titles
1	**New England Patriots** 6 Super Bowl Titles
3	**San Francisco 49ers** 5 Super Bowl Titles
3	**Dallas Cowboys** 5 Super Bowl Titles
5	**Green Bay Packers** 4 Super Bowl Titles
5	**New York Giants** 4 Super Bowl Titles

Pittsburgh Steelers quarterback Terry Bradshaw celebrated after winning Super Bowl XIV in 1980.

Worst to First

The worst run a team has had in NFL history goes to the Tampa Bay Buccaneers. As an **expansion team** in 1976, expectations weren't very high. But things went worse than expected, and the Bucs finished their first season 0–14. Tampa's woes continued the next season. They lost their first twelve games to run their losing streak to 26 straight games. The Bucs finally won their first game when they topped the New Orleans Saints 33–14 just before Christmas in 1977.

Long-suffering Buccaneer fans finally had something to cheer about in 2002. That year they made the playoffs for the fourth straight season. They capped it all off on January 26, 2003, by winning Super Bowl XXXVII under head coach Jon Gruden.

The quarterback for the winless 1976 Buccaneers team was Steve Spurrier. He later became a college football coach. In 1996 he coached the Florida Gators to win the national championship.

Worst Single-Season Team Record
(since the AFL-NFL merger in 1970)

TEAM	YEAR	RECORD
Tampa Bay Buccaneers	1976	0–14
Detroit Lions	2008	0–16
Cleveland Browns	2017	0–16

With coach Jon Gruden's leadership, the Tampa Bay Buccaneers won their first Super Bowl championship in 2003.

Tough Times in Buffalo

The Buffalo Bills had wonderful teams in the early 1990s. Behind star players like Jim Kelly, Thurman Thomas, Bruce Smith, and coach Marv Levy, they made it to four consecutive Super Bowls.

Unfortunately, they lost all four years. Following the 1990 season, the Bills lost the Super Bowl to the New York Giants 20–19 on a missed game-winning kick at the end. The next year they were beaten by Washington 37–24. The Dallas Cowboys had their number the next two years. They pummeled the Bills 52–17 and 30–13, respectively.

It was rough being a Bills fan. But on the bright side, no other team has ever made it to the Super Bowl in four consecutive seasons.

Most Super Bowl Losses

TEAM	NUMBER OF SUPER BOWL LOSSES
Denver Broncos	5
New England Patriots	5
Minnesota Vikings	4
Buffalo Bills	4

The Buffalo Bills seemed to be cursed as they lost four straight Super Bowls from 1991 to 1994.

SUPER BOWL GAMES AND WINNERS

I   Jan. 15, 1967 – Green Bay 35, Kansas City 10

II   Jan. 14, 1968 – Green Bay 33, Oakland 14

III   Jan. 12, 1969 – New York Jets 16, Baltimore 7

IV   Jan. 11, 1970 – Kansas City 23, Minnesota 7

V   Jan. 17, 1971 – Baltimore 16, Dallas 13

VI   Jan. 16, 1972 – Dallas 24, Miami 3

VII   Jan. 14, 1973 – Miami 14, Washington 7

VIII   Jan. 13, 1974 – Miami 24, Minnesota 7

IX   Jan. 12, 1975 – Pittsburgh 16, Minnesota 6

X   Jan. 18, 1976 – Pittsburgh 21, Dallas 17

XI   Jan. 9, 1977 – Oakland 32, Minnesota 14

XII   Jan. 15, 1978 – Dallas 27, Denver 10

XIII   Jan. 21, 1979 – Pittsburgh 35, Dallas 31

XIV   Jan. 20, 1980 – Pittsburgh 31, LA Rams 19

XV   Jan. 25, 1981 – Oakland 27, Philadelphia 10

XVI   Jan. 24, 1982 – San Francisco 26, Cincinnati 21

XVII   Jan. 30, 1983 – Washington 27, Miami 17

XVIII   Jan. 22, 1984 – LA Raiders 38, Washington 9

XIX   Jan. 20, 1985 – San Francisco 38, Miami 16

XX   Jan. 26, 1986 – Chicago 46, New England 10

XXI   Jan. 25, 1987 – New York Giants 39, Denver 20

XXII   Jan. 31, 1988 – Washington 42, Denver 10

XXIII   Jan. 22, 1989 – San Francisco 20, Cincinnati 16

XXIV   Jan. 28, 1990 – San Francisco 55, Denver 10

XXV   Jan. 27, 1991 – New York Giants 20, Buffalo 19

XXVI   Jan. 26, 1992 – Washington 37, Buffalo 24

XXVII   Jan. 31, 1993 – Dallas 52, Buffalo 17

XXVIII   Jan. 30, 1994 – Dallas 30, Buffalo 13

XXIX	Jan. 29, 1995 – San Francisco 49, San Diego 26
XXX	Jan. 28, 1996 – Dallas 27, Pittsburgh 17
XXXI	Jan. 26, 1997 – Green Bay 35, New England 21
XXXII	Jan. 25, 1998 – Denver 31, Green Bay 24
XXXIII	Jan. 31, 1999 – Denver 34, Atlanta 19
XXXIV	Jan. 30, 2000 – St. Louis 23, Tennessee 16
XXXV	Jan. 28, 2001 – Baltimore 34, New York Giants 7
XXXVI	Feb. 3, 2002 – New England 20, St. Louis 17
XXXVII	Jan. 26, 2003 – Tampa Bay 48, Oakland 21
XXXVIII	Feb. 1, 2004 – New England 32, Carolina 29
XXXIX	Feb. 6, 2005 – New England 24, Philadelphia 21
XL	Feb. 5, 2006 – Pittsburgh 21, Seattle 10
XLI	Feb. 4, 2007 – Indianapolis 29, Chicago 17
XLII	Feb. 3, 2008 – New York Giants 17, New England 14
XLIII	Feb. 1, 2009 – Pittsburgh 27, Arizona 23
XLIV	Feb. 7, 2010 – New Orleans 31, Indianapolis 17
XLV	Feb. 6, 2011 – Green Bay 31, Pittsburgh 25
XLVI	Feb. 5, 2012 – New York Giants 21, New England 17
XLVII	Feb. 3, 2013 – Baltimore 34, San Francisco 31
XLVIII	Feb. 2, 2014 – Seattle 43, Denver 8
XLIX	Feb. 1, 2015 – New England 28, Seattle 24
50	Feb. 7, 2016 – Denver 24, Carolina 10
LI	Feb. 5, 2017 – New England 34, Atlanta 28 (OT)
LII	Feb. 4, 2018 – Philadelphia 41, New England 33
LIII	Feb. 3, 2019 – New England 13, Los Angeles Rams 3
LIV	Feb. 2, 2020 – Kansas City 31, San Francisco 20
LV	Feb. 7, 2021 – Tampa Bay 31, Kansas City 9

GLOSSARY

anticipation (an-tis-uh-PAY-shuhn)—expecting something to happen

concussion (kuhn-KUH-shuhn)—an injury to the brain caused by a hard blow to the head

consecutive (kuhn-SEK-yuh-tiv)—when something happens several times in a row without a break

dynasty (DYE-nuh-stee)—a team that wins multiple championships over a period of several years

expansion team (ik-SPAN-shuhn TEEM)—a new team that is added to an existing league

franchise (FRAN-chize)—a team that operates under the rules and regulations of a professional sports league or organization

interception (in-tur-SEP-shun)—a pass caught by a defensive player

ligament (LIG-uh-muhnt)—a strong band of tissue that connects bones to bones

pick six (PIK SIKS)—a touchdown scored off an interception by the defense

rookie (RUH-kee)—a first-year player

sack (SAK)—when a defensive player tackles the opposing quarterback behind the line of scrimmage

therapy (THER-uh-pee)—a treatment for an injury or disability

unique (yoo-NEEK)—one of a kind

upset (UP-set)—to be defeated by a team that was expected to lose

READ MORE

Chandler, Matt. *Football's Greatest Hail-Mary Passes and Other Crunch-time Heroics*. North Mankato, MN: Capstone Press, 2020.

Hetrick, Hans. *Football's Record Breakers*. North Mankato, MN: Capstone Press, 2017.

Jankowski, Matthew. *The Greatest Football Players of All Time*. New York: Gareth Stevens Publishing, 2020.

INTERNET SITES

Pro Football Hall of Fame
profootballhof.com/

Pro Football Reference
pro-football-reference.com

Sports Illustrated Kids
sikids.com

INDEX